F6

Six moves to build your foundation

Lee McCormack
Race Line Publishing : www.leelikesbikes.com

with Erin Carson
RallySport Health and Fitness : Boulder, CO

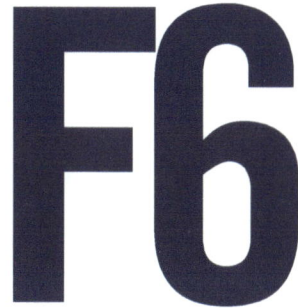

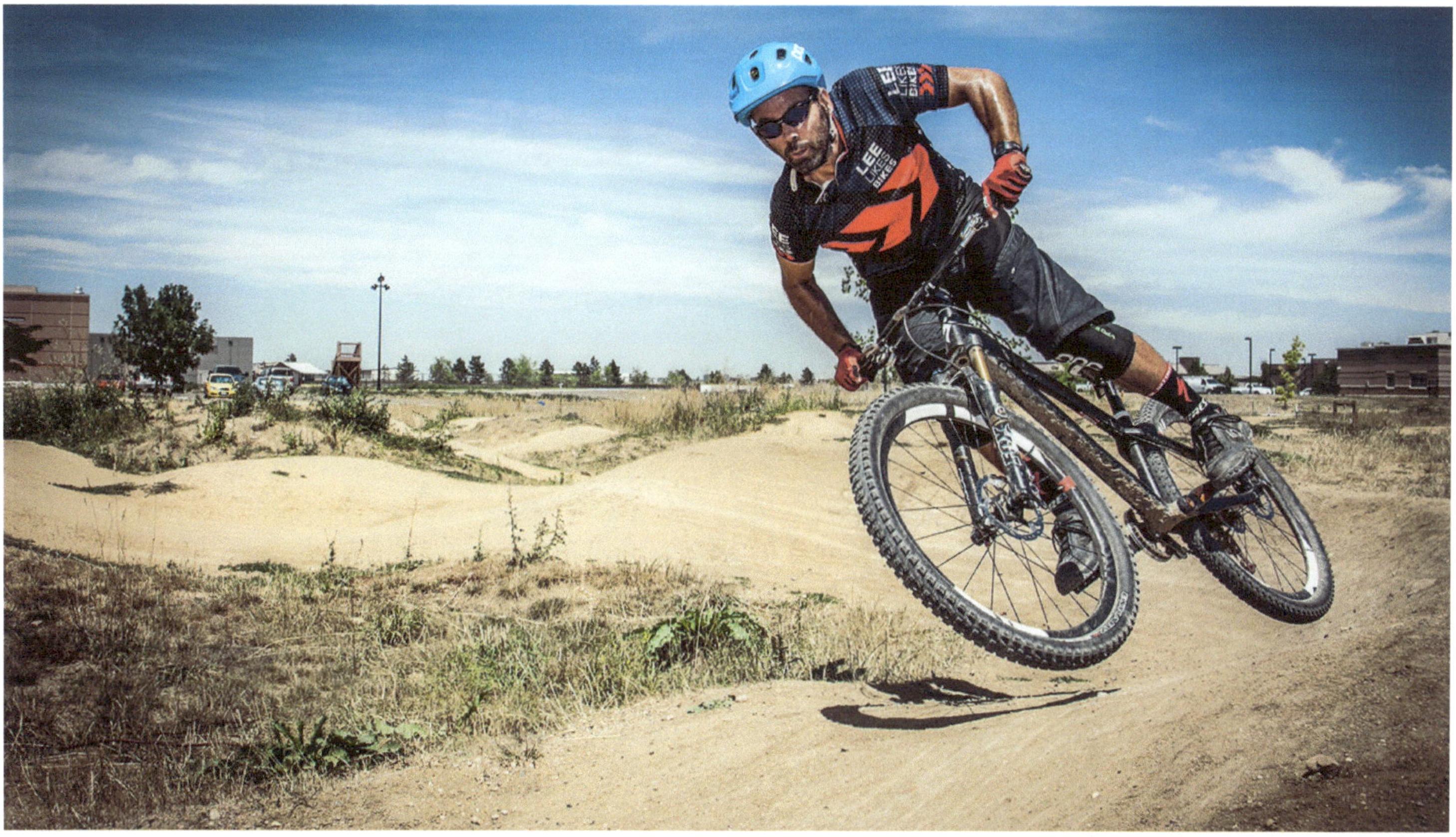

The F6 will help you pump corners so hard you fly right out of them.
Lee uses the squat row at Valmont Bike Park. Photo by yannphotovideo.com

LEE
LIKES
BIKES

ISBN-10: 0-9745660-6-3

Copyright © 2014 by Lee McCormack, Race Line Publishing. All rights reserved.

v1 Feb. 4 , 2014

All words and images by Lee McCormack unless otherwise noted.
Exercise photos by Arlette McCormack.
Photoshop cutouts by Farid Tabaian, Singletrack Maps.

Use of information
No part of this document may be used, reproduced, stored, recorded or transmitted in any form or manner whatsoever — including electronic distribution — without written permission from the copyright holder. To reserve such permission, contact Lee McCormack at lee@leelikesbikes.com

Disclaimer
Mountain biking and training for mountain biking are potentially dangerous. Race Line Publishing, Lee Likes Bikes LLC, the author and their associates assume no liability whatsoever for any damages associated in any way with the information contained herein. Before you start any workout program, check with your physician. If you have any questions or concerns, consult a qualified trainer near you.

PLEASE DO NOT STEAL THIS

It took a lot of time and effort to create this work.

Please do not send this book to friends, post it online, photocopy it,
share the video links/passwords or steal it in other ways.

Thank you very much. Now let's get strong!

-- Lee

This book is dedicated to my wife Arlette and our kids Kate (24), Ian (21) and the twins Finley and Fiona (4).

Finley and Fiona show Daddy around Valmont Bike Park.

Contents (click on a section to go there)

Quick start guide	6
Who is Lee McCormack?	7
Who is Erin Carson?	7
What is the F6?	8
Who is the F6 for?	9
What are we trying to accomplish?	10
One step at a time	11
Living with the F6	12
Required equipment	14
Learn the F6 moves	15
Squat row	15
Lunge swing	16
Dead row	17
Reach press	18
Hinge pull	19
Lunge push	20
Why these moves?	21
Let us help you	26
Big thanks to my sponsors	27

A fun way to use your strength. Lee very heavy then very light at Valmont Bike Park.

F6: Six moves to build your foundation : Lee McCormack : Race Line Publishing : www.leelikesbikes.com

The F6 fits into real life: Put your kids to bed and get after it.

Quick start guide

1. Squat row

2. Lunge swing

3. Dead row

>>> Do all six exercises in a circuit.

>>> 10 quality reps per set. No more than one minute per set.

>>> Perform one to three circuits. This should take 10-30 minutes.

4. Reach press

5. Hinge row

6. Lunge push

F6: Six moves to build your foundation : Lee McCormack : Race Line Publishing : www.leelikesbikes.com

Who is Lee McCormack?

Hi, I'm Lee McCormack and I like bikes.
Some things I do in the bike world:

>>> Run the site www.leelikesbikes.com

>>> Teach riding skills to riders of all types and levels, from beginners to pros.
Check out skills clinics with Lee.

>>> Wrote the books
Mastering Mountain Bike Skills,
Pro BMX Skills,
Teaching Mountain Bike Skills,
Pump Up the Base,
Prepare to Pin It and
Welcome to Pump Track Nation.

>>> As skills development director for the National Interscholastic Cycling Association, I create and teach the curricula used to train high school coaches and athletes throughout the United States.

>>> Design and build pump tracks and bike parks. Check out LLB design/build services.

>>> Decent all-around rider. Have I mentioned that I like bikes?

Last spring, after working with me for three years, master trainer Erin Carson gave me six exercises to keep me durable during my busy coaching/riding season. These movements have evolved to help my skills clients move and ride better. And here they are: The F6.

Who is Erin Carson?

Erin is the real deal as both an athlete and trainer.

She was an Olympic basketball player, and she is currently a top age-group long-distance triathlete. As the General Manager and Fitness Director for RallySport Health and Fitness in Boulder, CO, Erin works with all types of athletes, from housewives and weekend warriors to top pros. Last off season she trained me with national downhill champion Alex Willie.

Learn more about Erin on the RallySport website.
http://rallysportboulder.com/content/personal-training/index.php

What is the F6?

The F6 is a six-move circuit to help you:

- >>> Stay more balanced in gnarly terrain. Both up and down.
- >>> Carve corners tighter and faster.
- >>> Pump, manual and jump better.
- >>> Sprint and climb more powerfully.
- >>> Ride longer and faster on crazier terrain — with less fatigue and injury.

While you're getting stronger on the bike, you'll also be getting stronger for moving day, the airport and other real-life adventures.

The F6 is:

- >>> Simple. But not easy.
- >>> Quick. Do it in 10, 20 or 30 minutes.
- >>> Scalable. Anyone can adjust the program to his or her needs.
- >>> Made for real people who love to ride. Spend a little time learning great movement. Spend the rest of your time shredding!

Lunge push with a band anchored to my Sprinter van. Perfect at the trailhead or in my driveway.

F6: Six moves to build your foundation : Lee McCormack : Race Line Publishing : www.leelikesbikes.com

Who is the F6 for?

You love to ride. You are a mountain biker, and you should ride your bike. The F6 fits right into your current riding or training schedule.

You want to ride better. The better you can move, the better you can ride. Period.

You are busy. The F6 takes as little as 10 minutes, and you can do it pretty much anywhere. A full workout takes 20-30 minutes.

You are healthy and relatively uninjured. No matter who you are, start easy and work your way up. If you have any question about your ability to rock F6 safely, see a health care professional or qualified trainer.

You don't want to commit to long-term off-bike training program. Those programs can be very effective, but they only work if you have the time, disposition and energy to follow them. If/when you decide to start a more comprehensive training program, the F6 will help you be ready.

> **If you want a complete strength training program** designed for mountain bikers, check out Enduro MTB Training.

When the trail drops away, you need to get low and actively push your bike down. The F6 gives you the balance, range of motion and strength to shred like 2012 national downhill champion Alex Willie, who worked with Lee for years.

What are we trying to accomplish?

As you learn the six exercises in the F6 training program, you will:

Ride better. As a skills instructor, I've worked with more than 1,000 riders of all levels — from beginners to pros — and most of them have the same instability, tightness and weakness. The F6 will give you a solid foundation for ripping.

Live better. The F6 moves are tailored to the demands of mountain biking, but moving is moving. You'll be stronger and safer everywhere.

Actually be able to do the program. The best fitness program is the one you actually do. Not the one that happens at the gym you never visit, nor the one that's locked in a bunch of confusing PDFs. The F6 is simple, infinitely scalable and can be done almost anywhere in as few as 10 minutes.

Not hurt yourself. The F6 is all about learning to move. As you master these movements you'll gradually add difficulty, range of motion and resistance. Be patient and careful.

Have plenty of energy for riding. If you were the kind of person who wants to live in the gym, you'd be there already. The F6 will not beat you down. You are a mountain biker: Your hardest workouts should be on the bike.

Learn how to stay balanced, then pull and push over big rocks.

As you bring the F6 to your bike, you will:

Maintain a lower, more balanced attack position (see the books Mastering Mountain Bike Skills, Pro BMX Skills, and Teaching Mountain Bike Skills). Spend more time closer to that microscopic place of perfect balance. Heavy feet, light hands!

Give beautiful violence to the trail. From your low, balanced position, you can create big angles and pump terrain like crazy.

Handle violence. When violence comes your way (hey, it happens), the F6 will help you stay balanced and keep rocking. Feel less tired and sore after rides. Reduce injuries.

Unlock your potential. Most of you have no idea how strong you actually are. Power is getting lost somewhere — usually between your hips and shoulders. As you master the F6, your brain will sense your greater capability and unleash more power for both pedaling and bike handling. Braaap!

One step at a time

The F6 is not the classic meathead "I gotta bench 300 so girls like me" weightlifting program that I pursued in my youth. For the sake of your safety, not to mention your performance and awesomeness, please follow these edicts:

Stability is job #1. You know you're stable when your hips, torso and shoulders are all tied together. Your hips point where you're going, and they stay level with the horizon. You maintain alignment and balance without wiggling around, leaning on your bars or falling over. When you are stable, you are safe. Do not add range or resistance until you're stable where you are!

Then comes mobility. Once you're stable in a particular position, then you can begin to expand your range. Get lower, reach farther, etc. As a bike skills instructor, I'm here to tell you: The more range of motion you have — while staying balanced on your pedal(s) — the more you can do on your bike.

Then comes strength. Once you're stable and mobile in a particular exercise, then it's time to add resistance. This might mean more weight or a firmer exercise band. The right amount of resistance is totally relative. You should feel the connections throughout your body. You should feel like you're working. But you must maintain great form. You should not push anywhere near failure, nor should you beat yourself up. Save your most violent workouts for the bike.

>>> If you want to lift heavier on a particular day, do a simpler, more stable version of the exercise.

Finally comes power. Power comes from stability, mobility and strength — plus speed. When your brain senses instability, tightness and weakness, it retards your muscles so you don't hurt yourself. This is happening on every ride, and you don't even know it. As you master the F6 and your brain senses that your system is ready, you'll notice yourself pumping faster, hopping higher, climbing more easily and sprinting harder. Pretty sweet.

Conrad Stoltz, four-time XTERRA World Champion, is one of the most talented people I've ever worked with. After some movement drills without weight, he was carving!

Photo by Liezel Stoltz.

Living with the F6

You'll be doing six movements. They are complex by design. Just learning the moves will be challenging (and awesome).

Each movement can be adjusted to suit your fitness, mobility, strength, tiredness, tightness or mood. Start simple. Add complexity and resistance after you master a certain level. These moves are challenging! I've been working on them for more than five years, and I'm still learning. Paint the fence, Daniel-san.

Alter your stance. Most of the exercises can use three different stances. Start with wide stance and work your way through bike stance and finally into single leg stance.

> **Wide stance:** Feet next to each other, toes pointing forward. This is the easiest and most stable option. Start here.
>
> > **Level 1:** Feet shoulder width apart.
> >
> > **Level 2:** As you get stronger, bring your feet closer together. When you can execute with your feet next to each other, start learning the bike stance.

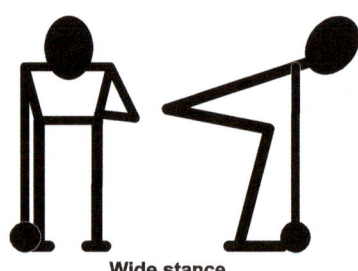

> **Bike stance:** Feet staggered with rear toe just behind front heel (you can start with more foot overlap). Width should mimic the side-to-side distance between your pedals.
>
> > **Level 1:** Front foot flat on the ground. Most of your weight on the front foot. Lift your rear heel as needed.
> >
> > **Level 2:** Both feet flat on the ground and equally weighted. This is hard! But it'll help you stay balanced on the bike, especially on gnarly downhills.

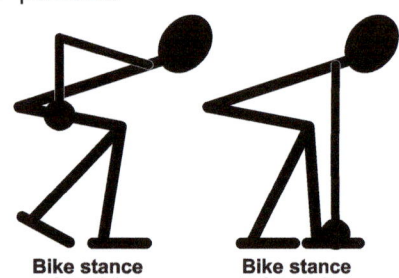

> **Single foot stance:** Stand on one foot. Keep your hips pointing forward and level with the horizon. Don't let your non-standing hip slump downward. This is hard, especially with heavy dead rows.
>
> > **Level 1:** Hang your non-standing leg wherever you need for balance.
> >
> > **Level 2:** As you get stronger, keep your non-standing leg closer to you. Strive to keep your knees next to each other. This'll keep you busy!

Learn to lunge: Lunges open your hips and counteract every cyclist's tendency to curl into a ball. Keep the forward knee over your foot. Extend the rear leg as much as possible, while keeping your hips pointing forward and your torso upright.

Perform all six exercises in a circuit. Strive for 10 quality reps per set, with a maximum of one minute per set. If you're using bike, single leg or lunge stance, do one set with each foot. For example:

    Squat row, wide stance - 1 set
    Lunge swing - 2 sets
    Dead row, single leg - 2 sets
    Reach press, single leg - 2 sets
    Hinge pull, wide stance - 1 set
    Lunge push - 2 sets
    TOTAL - 10 sets

> **If something hurts, stop!**
> Working hard is good.
> Hurting yourself is bad.
> Pay attention to form.
> Listen to your body!

One circuit takes about 10 minutes. Two sets take about 20 minutes. Three take about 30 minutes. Rest as needed: ideally when you're done.

Try to do at least one circuit every day, especially while you are learning the moves. A light round is a great way to loosen up for a ride (or while you're stuck in the office).

Do two rounds at least twice a week. Two quality rounds are plenty of work, especially if you rode that day. Hit the F6 right after you ride.

Three rounds is a full workout. If you're not riding that day, make F6x3 your training focus. Warm up however you like. Drill it for 30 minutes.

If you really suck at a movement, practice it as often as you can. If you have kids, pick up socks and toys on one foot, with perfect form.

When you can do 10 reps with perfect form, add a circuit. When you're doing all the circuits you want with perfect form, increase resistance: Add five pounds to your weight and step up to the next color band.

Spend the rest of your life learning to move better. As you master the F6, add range, resistance or other challenges. Heck, one of my skills clients does the single-leg exercises on a Bosu ball. Focus on whatever challenges you. Be consistent. Have fun!

Integrate the F6 into your rides and/or on-bike training program. May I suggest these simple, effective programs:

    Pump Up the Base - 12-week off-season base and speed building program. $14.99 ebook.

    Prepare to Pin It - 12-week in-season training program for endurance and speed. $19.99 ebook.

    Tip: If you're training hard on and off the bike, try doing the F6 right after your bike workout. Take it easy the next day.

F6: Six moves to build your foundation : Lee McCormack : Race Line Publishing : www.leelikesbikes.com

Required equipment

This program is designed to work most places with whatever you have available. Do it in the gym, your garage, at your car after a ride (ideal), at a rest stop, in a hotel room or at your office. Be creative.

All you need is:

>>> Something to pull and push

>>> Something to lift

In the gym

>>> Pull and push: Cable machine

>>> Lift: Dumbbells, kettlebells, Sandbells or whatever they have

Out of the gym

>>> Pull and push: Exercise bands or surgical tubing. Tubing works fine, but it snaps catastrophically. I know this!

Check out Lifeline Professional Exercise Tubing w/Handles at PerformBetter.com.

>>> Lift: Dumbbells (adjustable ones are ideal), rocks, bricks, sandbags, milk jugs filled with water, etc. Kids get heavier every day, and they love to be lifted.

"**Light**" might be 5-15 pounds.

"**Heavy**" might be 10+ pounds. On a strong day I can dead row 75 pounds, but I usually use 15-60.

Lots of good lifting options at PerformBetter.com.

Remember: F6 is all about quality movement. Weight isn't nearly as important as balance, range and alignment. Be careful.

Trainer Gerett Burl reaches with a ViPR at RallySport Health and Fitness in Boulder, CO. Gyms have lots of fun toys.

Rock the F6 anywhere with surgical tubing, adjustable dumbbell and a handlebar (optional, to make squat rows and lunge pushes more bike specific).

Learn the F6 moves

F6 moves are complex, and most riders find them tricky. Start with the easiest stance and very light weight. Move only as far as you can with good alignment. Increase the challenge — trickier stance, more range and greater resistance — as you learn the moves.

1. Squat row

Equipment: Cable or band

Stances: Wide, bike, single

Cues:

>>> Chest high

>>> Hips square: aligned with torso, forward, level

>>> Drive hips and hands together — at the same time.

Wide stance:

Bike stance

Single leg stance

Video: https://vimeo.com/85870598
Password: effsixstrong!

F6: Six moves to build your foundation : Lee McCormack : Race Line Publishing : www.leelikesbikes.com

2. Lunge swing

Equipment: Light weights, one in each hand

Stance: Lunge

Cues:

>>> Open the front of your body. Elevate your rib cage.

>>> Strive for a rhythmic swing.

>>> Intentionally drive the weights upward *and* downward.

A gallon of water weighs eight pounds.

Reach up
Lift as high as you can.

Feel a stretch on the front of your body

Reach back

Knee above foot

Video: https://vimeo.com/85870599
Password: effsixstrong!

3. Dead row

Equipment: Heavy weight in one hand

Stances: Wide, bike, single

Cues:

>>> Push your hips back.

>>> Hips and torso in line. No bending or twisting.

>>> Make you torso as long as you can.

Single leg stance:

The dead row is an evolution of the single legged deadlift, which I learned from trainer James Wilson.

Video: https://vimeo.com/85870600
Password: effsixstrong!

4. Reach press

Equipment: Light weight in one hand

Stances: Wide, bike, single

Cues:

>>> Push your hips back. Hips and torso in line. Try not to bend or twist at the waist.

>>> Alternate sides. As you get stronger, reach farther away from you. Hold the weight away from your torso as you press upward.

>>> When you are ready, turn your hips to the side you're reaching to (see below). This is like railing a flat corner.

Single leg with a hip turn:

If your knee hurts, stop!

The movement should happen in your ankle and hip.

Video: https://vimeo.com/85870602
Password: effsixstrong!

5. Hinge pull

Equipment: Cable or band

Stances: Wide, bike, single

Cues:

>>> Push your hips back. Shoulders as low as you can get 'em (probably lower than mine).

>>> Hips and torso in line. No bending or twisting. Stable core.

>>> As you get stronger, keep your hands farther to the side. A handlebar adds realism.

Bike stance:

Stable torso

Strong pull

Wide stance: *Single leg stance:*

This is challenging!

Video: https://vimeo.com/85870605
Password: effsixstrong!

6. Lunge push

Equipment: Cable or band

Stance: Lunge

Cues:

>>> Hips and torso in line.

>>> Chest high. Open the front of your body.

>>> Try to move your hands and foot at the same time.
As you get stronger, lunge more deeply and hold your hands farther out to the sides.
A handlebar (preferably the same Shimano PRO you run on your bikes) adds realism.

Push with hands

Torso upright

Reach with foot

Video: https://vimeo.com/85870614
Password: effsixstrong!

Turbo options:

>>> These variations add challenge to squat rows, hinge rows and lunge pushes.

>>> Hold your hands farther out to the sides. For added realism, attach the bands to a handlebar (preferably the same Shimano PRO bar you use on all your bikes).

>>> With bike and single leg stance, pull or push with one arm at a time.
Do five reps with one arm, then switch arms. After that, switch feet then do five reps with each arm.

F6: Six moves to build your foundation : Lee McCormack : Race Line Publishing : www.leelikesbikes.com

Why these moves?

I hope you'll find confidence and stoke knowing this program is designed specifically for your needs as a mountain biker — by a skills instructor who's intimately familiar with how mountain bikers should move.
As a reminder, here are the overall goals for the F6:

>>> Enhance core stability, upper body pull and lower body push, which are critical to MTB (and many other sports).

>>> Counteract common mobility issues cyclists face.

>>> No gym needed. Very little equipment needed.

>>> Get as many things done in as short a time possible.

Here are the specific reasons for each F6 move:

Applying squat-row skill to a double manual. Check out the video!

Squat row

Many sports — including cross country skiing, rowing and of course mountain biking — are powered by upper body pull and lower body push. This power should come from your back and butt.

In my skills clinics, I teach riders how to control their bikes with their upper bodies, then I teach them how to make power with their lower bodies. When these movements start to look good, I teach the riders how to unite them. Once a rider gets this connection, it's game on — both uphill and downhill.

The squat row teaches you how to combine upper body pull with lower body push. This is the most powerful movement pattern we humans have, and it's at the heart of a lot of fun stuff: sprinting, technical climbing, wheelie drops, pumping, manualing, jumping and more.

The squat row will revolutionize your climbing, especially up rocks and ledges. Middle photo by yannphotovideo.com. Right photo: Skills client Ksenia Lepikhina carries more speed with less effort.

Lunge swing

If you spend a lot of time sitting — at a desk, in your car and on your bike — you need to work the opposite movement. We cyclists have notoriously tight hip flexors, which contribute to various discomforts including low back pain.

Reach back with your leg and up with your arms. Make the front of your body as long as possible. While you're at it, you're opening your hips and strengthening your core and back. Yogis will be reminded of Warrior 1, which is pretty much the opposite of hunching at your desk on or your bike. *Warrior 1 yoga photo from run.com.*

Dead row

As Rider (capital R), you should spend a lot of time in your low attack position: weight on your feet (or foot), hips back, shoulders low. From here, you'll control the bike with your upper body and create power from your hips.

The dead row combines a bent row with a dead lift. The row part teaches you to pull hard with your arms while keeping your torso still. The dead lift part teaches you to create power from your hips (while keeping your torso long and straight). At the same time, the dead row helps you stabilize from your core.
All good stuff for shredding.

Learn more about riding position in these Lee Likes Bikes books.

*Photo: It takes a strong core and a powerful pull to skim over a big roller. Pro XC racer and Lee Likes Bikes skills client Judy Freeman squashes backsides and skips frontsides at Valmont Bike Park.
Photo by yannphotovideo.com.*

Reach press

To carve turns, you need to balance on your feet (or foot), get your torso low then lean your bike independently from your body. Meanwhile, you need to stay balanced while your bike is hitting things, drifting and goodness knows what else.

The reach press helps you with:

Lowness. Yeah, I know you just did dead rows. Lowness is important! Get strong, supple and balanced here.

Reach. While you're building a more centered, more stable base of support, you're also learning to move your bike farther away from your center. Sometimes you put your bike out there; sometimes it bounces out there. Either way, you'll be ready.

Rotation. To shred trails, you need to drive your hips and torso where you want to go. The reach press gives you that range of motion (while improving your balance and control).

Durability. More core strength is always good. Overhead push strength can help save you in a crash.

Practice huge range of motion with the F6, then carve corners well within your comfort zone. Photo by yannphotovideo.com.

After practicing movement off the bike, four-time XTERRA world champion Conrad Stoltz makes angles in a skills session with Lee. Photo by Liezel Stoltz.

Conrad Stoltz skills clinic with Lee McCormack : Aug. 3, 2012
www.leelikesbikes.com : Photos by Liezel Wium-Stoltz

Hinge pull

When your front wheel hits something — a roller, rock, log or whatever — your bars are gonna crash toward you. Most riders (lower case r) rely on their bike to absorb some of the hit, then brace themselves for the rest of the impact.

Real Riders (capital R) stay centered and actively make the bike do things. If your bars are about to get knocked toward you, don't wait for that to happen. Instead, stay balanced and PULL the bars toward you.

The hinge pull teaches you how to stay low and balanced while generating massive pull forces. This is the A1 key to minimizing catastrophic impacts.

Plus: This rowing motion helps you pump down backsides, for example rocks, rollers and dirt jump landings.

Whether you're coasting or pedaling, use balance, stability and pulling strength to ride over things things smoothly and efficiently. Left photo by Cody Waite. Right photo by Yosei Ikeda.

Lunge push

Riders (capital R) don't *let* their bikes do things.

Riders *make* their bikes do things.

When you ride off a rock, your bars are gonna fall away from you. Don't wait for your bike to pull you into the backside. Instead, stay balanced and *push* your bike into the backside.

The lunge push develops your pushing strength while strengthening your core and opening your hips (see lunge swing).

All good stuff for shredding.

Pushing down a rock and pushing off a drop require the same balance, range and strength. Lee Likes Bikes skills client and elite XC racer Judy Freeman shreds!

Left photo by Extreme Photography Unlimited.
Right photo by Lee (during a skills session at Valmont Bike Park).

Let us help you

As we've said, the F6 moves are challenging by design. You can figure them out by yourself, but a professional will help you learn faster and avoid bad habits and injuries.

In Boulder, CO

>>> **Let's rock a skills clinic!** I'll teach you the F6 and show you how the movements translate into better riding. This is the fastest way to achieve your riding goals. Check out **skills clinics with Lee** or email lee@leelikesbikes.com.

>>> **Contact Erin Carson** or any of the professional trainers at RallySport Health and Fitness.

Worldwide

I can help you with F6 and riding skills via email, phone, photos, video and/or Skype. Book an **LLB F6 Coaching Session** ($175 via Paypal). Questions? Email lee@leelikesbikes.com

Dee Tidwell is a highly respected trainer who specializes in mountain bike fitness. His company Enduro MTB Training offers:

Dee at his gym with my custom Fix the Broken Guy program.

>>> A complete six-month downloadable training program for enduro and trail riders.

>>> One-on-one coaching in Greenwood Village, CO.

>>> Personalized remote coaching.

Special Enduro MTB Training F6 program:

>>> Access to Dee via phone, email, phone, photos, video and/or Skype.

>>> Dee will help you with all six F6 moves.

>>> Dee will identify mobility issues and help you fix them. Don't be surprised if he reveals some major problems, I mean "opportunities."

>>> **$99**. **Pay here via Paypal**, and Dee will contact you. Be sure to include a current email address.

Big thanks to my sponsors

Specialized : specialized.com

In 2002 I started riding with the Specialized crew, and I learned: 1) these guys rip!, 2) they are super passionate about building great bikes! and 3) they know how to build great bikes!

I've been a Specialized guy ever since, and I really appreciate my beautiful quiver:

- **2014 S-Works Enduro 29** mega trail slayer
  Shimano XTR/XT drivetrain, brakes and pedals. PRO cockpit. Gamut Dual P20s chain guide.
- **2014 Stumpjumper Expert Carbon HT World Cup** rigid carbon light saber
  Shimano XT drivetrain, brakes and pedals. PRO cockpit.
- **2014 Enduro SX** slalom bike
  FOX 831 fork and Float CTD shock. Shimano XT drivetrain, wheels and brakes. Saint pedals. PRO cockpit. Gamut P20 chain guide.
- **2012 Stumpjumper FSR Expert Carbon 29** all-around tool of awesome (pictured)
  FOX 34 fork and RP23 shock. Shimano XTR/XT drivetrain, brakes and pedals. PRO cockpit.
- **2012 P3** dirt jump bike
  FOX 831 fork. Shimano XT drivetrain, wheels and brakes. PRO cockpit. Saint pedals. Gamut P20 chain guide.
- **2012 Demo 8** downhill sled
  FOX 40 fork. Shimano Saint drivetrain, brakes, chain guide and pedals. PRO cockpit.
- **2008 S-Works Tricross** cyclocross/training machine
  Shimano Ultegra SL drivetrain. XT pedals.

Shimano : bike.shimano.com

I've been a Shimano lover since I was 10, when I got a Shimano ultralight spinning reel for Christmas. 34 years later that tiny reel has handled trout, bass, catfish, seabass, bonito, yellowtail, dorado and even small tuna — and it's still rocking.

Shimano bike components bring the same level of rock-solid performance, reliability and longevity. My bikes have a mix of XTR, XT, Saint and PRO components. I love the consistent feel, and just *knowing* they are going to work for me. **Warning:** After you try Shimano Ice Tech brakes, you won't be able to tolerate anything else.

FOX : ridefox.com

Professional quality suspension made by passionate professionals. FOX suspension has never, not once, let me down, and it gives me the confidence to ride at my best.

The Fix Bike Shop : thefixbikes.com

My favorite shop in Boulder, CO. Full stock of braaap-friendly bikes, components and accessories, plus the know-how and coolness to dial you in. Located right next to the Valmont Bike Park.

Gamut USA : gamutusa.com Elegant, reliable chain guides.
POC Sports : pocsports.com MIPS helmets plus gloves and pads.

Almost done. The wine belongs to my wife Arlette, the photographer. Really!